ZODIAC MANDALAS

Color by Number

Celestial Patterns and Astrology Coloring Book for Adults with Suns, Moons, Stars, Planets and Constellations

Copyright © 2022

Thank you for your purchase!

Claim your FREE digital copy of our Highlight Reel Color By Number Book:

Check out our website: colorquestopia.com

Join our Facebook group:
facebook.com/colorquestopia

Follow us on Instagram: @colorquestopia

Did you enjoy this book?
Please leave us a review!

https://geni.us/cqreview

Our Color Palette Tips

1. **Colors corresponding to each number are shown on the back cover of the book. There are 25 colors total in this book, including one "Flesh Tone" color where you can choose any flesh tone!**
   Each number corresponds to a color shown on the back of the book. **There will sometimes be an asterisk (*) that corresponds to "Any Flesh Tone."**
   To the left of each image, there's a list of colors used within that particular image. Simply match the numbers on the images to the colors on the list. If you tear a page out of the book, you can simply use the color key on the back of the book to match your colors. If you don't have an exact color match, that's totally fine. Feel free to use a similar color or shade. Although this is a color by number book, it's completely okay to get creative and change up the colors listed. You can let your imagination run wild, and color the images with whichever colors you like and have. The numbers are here to be a guide and to allow you to color without having to focus your energy on choosing colors.

2. **If there are any spaces on an image without a number, you can go ahead and leave that space white (blank)**
   You can leave any space without a number white (blank), or you can fill that space in with any color you like. Another idea is to color that space in with a white color (for example, if you'd like to use a shiny white or a different shade of white on an image.)

3. **Bonus Images may have a slightly different color palette**
   Because the bonus images are from previous books with slightly different color palettes, they may include colors that aren't on the back of this book. Simply match them the best that you can, or choose completely different colors if you like. You are the artist and you are allowed to relax and enjoy!

Color By Number Tips

1. **Relax and have fun**

   Let your cares slip away as you color the images. Take your time. Coloring is a meditative activity and there's no wrong way to do it. Feel free to color as you listen to music, watch TV, lounge in bed- do whatever relaxes you most! You can also color while you're out and about- on the train or at a cafe- take the book with you anywhere you go. Coloring is therapeutic and is great for stress relief and relaxation!

2. **Choose your coloring tools**

   Everyone has their favorite coloring markers, crayons, pencils, pens- even paints! Feel free to color with any tool that you like! If you choose markers or paints, **we recommend putting a blank sheet of paper or cardboard behind each image, so that your colors don't run onto the next image.**

3. **Test out your colors**

   Feel free to test out your colors on our Color Test Sheets at the back, and use our Custom Color Chart to make the color choices your own!

   Relax and Enjoy!

7. Peach

8. Red

11. Light Yellow

12. Yellow

15. Green

17. Aqua Green

20. Dark Blue

22. Violet

23. Pink

24. Vivid Pink

1. Black

4. Brown

5. Dark Brown

8. Red

10. Orange

12. Yellow

14. Light Green

15. Green

19. Blue

20. Dark Blue

21. Lilac

22. Violet

23. Pink

24. Vivid Pink

1. Black

4. Brown

5. Dark Brown

6. Tan

7. Peach

8. Red

10. Orange

12. Yellow

18. Light Blue

19. Blue

20. Dark Blue

22. Violet

24. Vivid Pink

*. Any Flesh Tone

1. Black

4. Brown

5. Dark Brown

6. Tan

7. Peach

9. Orange Red

10. Orange

12. Yellow

15. Green

18. Light Blue

19. Blue

20. Dark Blue

24. Vivid Pink

*. Any Flesh Tone

1. Black

7. Peach

8. Red

9. Orange Red

10. Orange

11. Light Yellow

12. Yellow

14. Light Green

15. Green

19. Blue

20. Dark Blue

22. Violet

23. Pink

24. Vivid Pink

✻. Any Flesh Tone

2. Gray

3. Dark Gray

9. Orange Red

10. Orange

12. Yellow

14. Light Green

15. Green

17. Aqua Green

18. Light Blue

20. Dark Blue

22. Violet

24. Vivid Pink

1. Black

5. Dark Brown

8. Red

10. Orange

12. Yellow

14. Light Green

15. Green

17. Aqua Green

18. Light Blue

19. Blue

20. Dark Blue

21. Lilac

22. Violet

24. Vivid Pink

7. Peach

8. Red

9. Orange Red

13. Golden Yellow

15. Green

16. Dark Green

18. Light Blue

19. Blue

20. Dark Blue

22. Violet

24. Vivid Pink

7. Peach

8. Red

9. Orange Red

10. Orange

12. Yellow

14. Light Green

15. Green

17. Aqua Green

18. Light Blue

19. Blue

20. Dark Blue

21. Lilac

22. Violet

23. Pink

24. Vivid Pink

1. Black

5. Dark Brown

8. Red

10. Orange

12. Yellow

16. Dark Green

18. Light Blue

19. Blue

21. Lilac

22. Violet

23. Pink

24. Vivid Pink

∗. Any Flesh Tone

1. Black

8. Red

9. Orange Red

10. Orange

11. Light Yellow

12. Yellow

14. Light Green

15. Green

18. Light Blue

20. Dark Blue

22. Violet

23. Pink

24. Vivid Pink

4. Brown

7. Peach

8. Red

9. Orange Red

10. Orange

12. Yellow

13. Golden Yellow

14. Light Green

15. Green

16. Dark Green

18. Light Blue

19. Blue

21. Lilac

22. Violet

23. Pink

24. Vivid Pink

1. Black

4. Brown

9. Orange Red

10. Orange

12. Yellow

14. Light Green

15. Green

16. Dark Green

18. Light Blue

20. Dark Blue

21. Lilac

22. Violet

23. Pink

24. Vivid Pink

1. Black

4. Brown

5. Dark Brown

8. Red

9. Orange Red

12. Yellow

14. Light Green

15. Green

16. Dark Green

17. Aqua Green

18. Light Blue

20. Dark Blue

22. Violet

24. Pink

1. Black

8. Red

10. Orange

11. Light Yellow

12. Yellow

13. Golden Yellow

14. Light Green

15. Green

19. Blue

20. Dark Blue

21. Lilac

22. Violet

24. Vivid Pink

∗. Any Flesh Tone

5. Dark Brown

6. Tan

8. Red

10. Orange

12. Yellow

13. Golden Yellow

15. Green

18. Light Blue

19. Blue

22. Violet

23. Pink

24. Vivid Pink

8. Red

9. Orange Red

10. Orange

11. Light Yellow

12. Yellow

13. Golden Yellow

14. Light Green

15. Green

17. Aqua Green

18. Light Blue

19. Blue

20. Dark Blue

23. Pink

24. Vivid Pink

1. Black

8. Red

10. Orange

12. Yellow

13. Golden Yellow

15. Green

17. Aqua Green

18. Light Blue

20. Dark Blue

21. Lilac

22. Violet

23. Pink

24. Vivid Pink

＊. Any Flesh Tone

1. Black

4. Brown

5. Dark Brown

6. Tan

8. Red

9. Orange Red

10. Orange

12. Yellow

15. Green

16. Dark Green

17. Aqua Green

18. Light Blue

19. Blue

21. Lilac

22. Violet

24. Vivid Pink

* . Any Flesh Tone

1. Black

4. Brown

5. Dark Brown

10. Orange

14. Light Green

15. Green

19. Blue

20. Dark Blue

21. Lilac

22. Violet

23. Pink

1. Black

4. Brown

5. Dark Brown

8. Red

10. Orange

12. Yellow

15. Green

17. Aqua Green

18. Light Blue

19. Blue

20. Dark Blue

22. Violet

24. Vivid Pink

∗. Any Flesh Tone

1. Black

4. Brown

8. Red

10. Orange

11. Light Yellow

12. Yellow

14. Light Green

15. Green

17. Aqua Green

18. Light Blue

19. Blue

22. Violet

24. Vivid Pink

7. Peach

8. Red

9. Orange Red

11. Light Yellow

12. Yellow

14. Light Green

15. Green

17. Aqua Green

18. Light Blue

20. Dark Blue

23. Pink

24. Vivid Pink

8. Red

10. Orange

12. Yellow

13. Golden Yellow

14. Light Green

16. Dark Green

17. Aqua Green

18. Light Blue

21. Lilac

22. Violet

24. Vivid Pink

1. Black

6. Tan

8. Red

10. Orange

12. Yellow

13. Golden Yellow

14. Light Green

15. Green

18. Light Blue

19. Blue

22. Violet

ENJOY BONUS
IMAGES FROM SOME
OF OUR
OTHER FUN
COLOR BY NUMBER
BOOKS!

FIND ALL OF OUR
BOOKS
ON AMAZON

MANDALA
Color By Number
Anti Anxiety Coloring Book
For Adult Relaxation

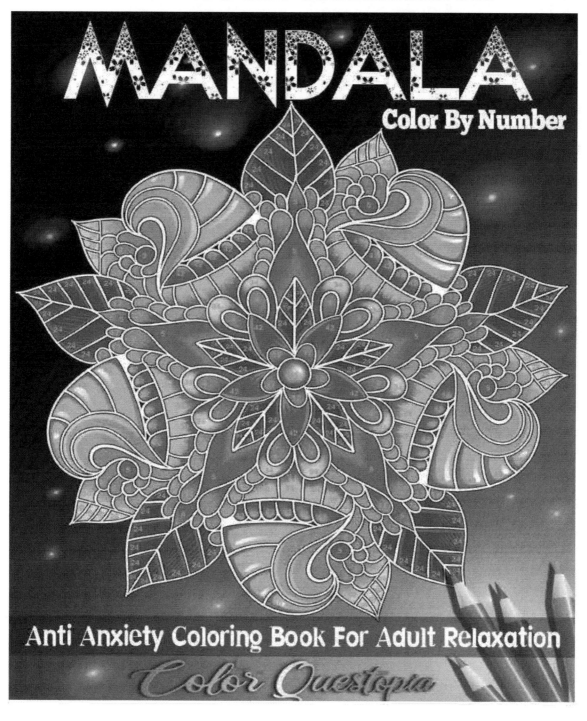

8. Red

9. Orange Red

12. Yellow

15. Green

17. Aqua Green

18. Light Blue

20. Dark Blue

23. Pink

24. Vivid Pink

Winter Mandalas
Color By Number
Coloring Book for Adults

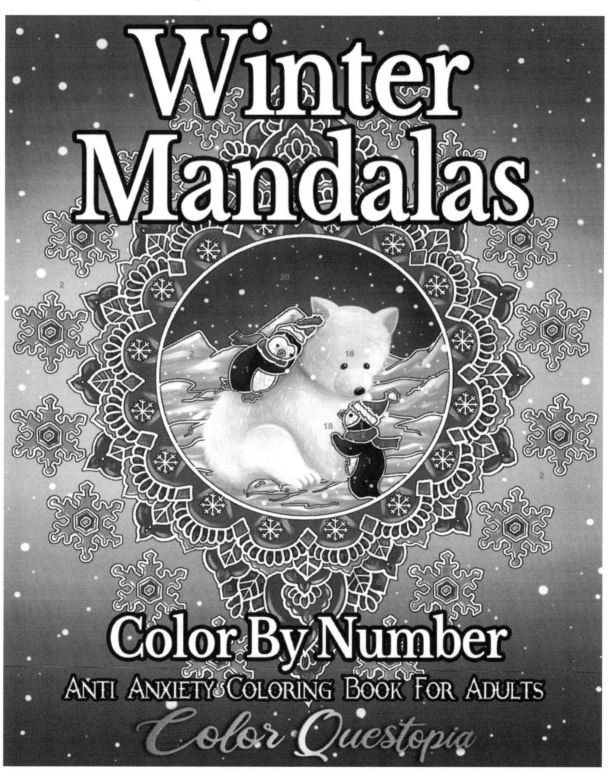

2. Gray

4. Brown

7. Peach

8. Red

9. Orange Red

10. Orange

11. Light Yellow

12. Yellow

14. Light Green

15. Green

16. Dark Green

18. Light Blue

19. Blue

20. Dark Blue

23. Pink

24. Vivid Pink

Dazzling Patterns
Color By Number
Anti Anxiety Coloring Book For Adults

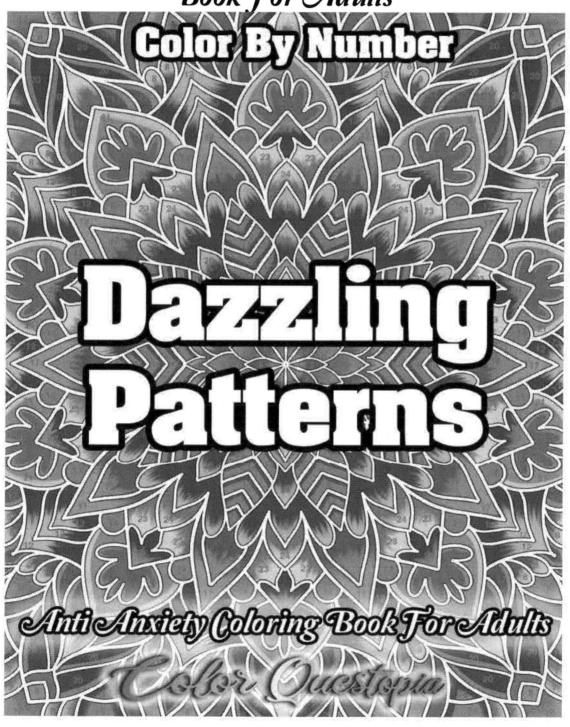

8. Red

10. Orange

12. Yellow

14. Light Green

17. Aqua Green

18. Light Blue

19. Blue

20. Dark Blue

22. Violet

23. Pink

24. Vivid Pink

SPACE COLORING BOOK

GALAXY COLOR BY NUMBER
FOR ADULTS AND KIDS OF ALL AGES

1. Blue

2. Light Yellow

3. Yellow

4. Light Orange

5. Orange

6. Medium Orange

7. Dark Orange

8. Navy Blue

9. Medium Brown

10. Brown

11. Light Brown

12. Dark Pink

13. Pink

14. Dark Yellow

15. Dark Brown

16. Light Blue

Delicious Food
Color By Number
Coloring Book for Adults

1. Black

2. Gray

4. Brown

5. Dark Brown

6. Tan

7. Peach

8. Red

10. Orange

11. Light Yellow

12. Yellow

13. Golden Yellow

15. Green

16. Dark Green

17. Aqua Green

18. Light Blue

19. Blue

Custom Color Chart

Medium: _ _ _ _ _ _ _ _   Brand: _ _ _ _ _ _ _ _

1. Black ____

2. Gray ____

3. Dark Gray ____

4. Brown ____

5. Dark Brown ____

6. Tan ____

7. Peach ____

8. Red ____

9. Orange Red ____

10. Orange ____

11. Light Yellow ____

12. Yellow ____

13. Golden Yellow ____

14. Light Green ____

15. Green ____

16. Dark Green ____

17. Aqua Green ____

18. Light Blue ____

19. Blue ____

20. Dark Blue ____

21. Lilac ____

22. Violet ____

23. Pink ____

24. Vivid Pink ____

* Flesh Tone ____

Custom Color Chart

Medium: _ _ _ _ _ _ _ _   Brand: _ _ _ _ _ _ _ _

1. _____

2. _____

3. _____

4. _____

5. _____

6. _____

7. _____

8. _____

9. _____

10. _____

11. _____

* 12. _____

13. _____

14. _____

15. _____

16. _____

17. _____

18. _____

19. _____

20. _____

21. _____

22. _____

23. _____

24. _____

* _____

Color Testing Sheet

Color Testing Sheet